Gratitude with Grace: Finding Happiness

Library of Congress Control Number: 2023916887

ISBN: 979-8-9884432-8-5 Hardcover
ISBN: 979-8-9884432-9-2 Paperback

Printed in the United States of America

Book cover designed by Achkouk
Edited by Alysha Welliver

https://AnitaFonteboa.com

Gratitude with Grace: Finding Happiness

Anita Fonteboa

DEDICATION

I dedicate this book to God, my angels, and my spiritual guides for inspiring me. Also, to my family for their support while I wrote this book. I spent many long nights typing, with you asking if I was done. I can now say I am. Lastly, I dedicate this book to you, to inspire you to be better.

SIGN UP FOR MY AUTHOR NEWSLETTER

Be one of the first to see Anita Fonteboa's new releases and get exclusive content tailored for both avid readers and aspiring writers!

HTTPS://ANITAFONTEBOA.COM

If you liked the book, please leave a brief review on websites like Amazon, Goodreads, Barnes & Noble, and other retailer's websites to support the author. Your valuable feedback can make a significant impact!

Table of Content

Dedications v

Introduction.. 1

Chapter 1- What is Gratitude? 7

Chapter 2 - What is Manifesting? 17

Chapter 3 - What is Intuition?................................ 29

Chapter 4 – Do You Know Your Words Have Power? 41

Chapter 5 – How to Change from Within? 51

Chapter 6 - What is Grounding? 63

Chapter 7- How is Meditation is Helpful?...................... 71

Chapter 8 - Finding Happiness 79

About the Author.. 89

Introduction

As I sat one day at my computer, this book flowed through my fingertips and onto my laptop. This book was born out of inspiration by my angels and guides. It is a catalyst for people to open themselves up to a new journey filled with mindfulness, gratitude, and change. Now, I am not a doctor or a therapist. I am intuitive and a psychic, however, I do not currently give readings.

While I am not a therapist, I took therapy to work on myself, and to see another side of me I could not see. Thanks to the advice given during therapy, I could make positive changes and become a better version of myself. In this way, I *"did me."* I'm here to encourage you to do the same. **DO YOU!**

You're about to start a journey of self-improvement and joy by connecting with a new mindset and exploring different ways of thinking and feeling, where fear no longer has a power over you but you have power over fear.

My life changed when I changed. By freeing myself from fear, I live a life of mindfulness and gratitude. I see things in a new light, appreciate them more fully, and radiate positivity and joy. Visualize yourself spreading joy, being surrounded by optimism, and accomplishing your dreams. Find your happiness by showing gratitude and being blessed with grace.

After my awakening, I gained a deeper understanding of gratitude's significance. My mission is to assist and inspire others to grow and uncover their path to happiness. Within these pages, you will gracefully unlock the art of infusing gratitude into your daily existence. You'll learn to harness intuition. By embracing nature, you will learn to shift negatives to positives and prioritize yourself in a challenging world. I will share wisdom from my personal experiences to help you improve yourself.

The first steps started when you decided you wanted to change. Please take a moment to get comfortable as you get engrossed with the new experiences. When you're ready, turn the page and let this chapter of self-discovery begin.

YOUR PEACE IS IMPORTANT. DO NOT GIVE IT AWAY TO THINGS THAT ARE NOT WORTH IT!

ASK FOR A SIGN! EITHER A FEATHER, RAINBOW, OR A BIRD. YOU WILL SEE IT!

POSITIVE, ALWAYS!

WHEN YOU FOCUS ON THE FUTURE, YOU MISS THE MOMENT YOU PRAYED FOR.

Chapter One

What is Gratitude?

Gratitude involves being thankful for the positive aspects of our lives and what we have in life. Appreciating the stuff we often overlook, such as having a home, food, clean water, loved ones, and even access to technology, can lighten your heart.

When was the last time you took a moment to give thanks? This is not a trick question. Though for some of you, it may be a hard question, as the thought never crossed your mind. That's okay, because now it has, and now you can do it. All it takes is just one to five minutes of your time each day. It can be as simple as saying a prayer or writing it on paper.

When you show grace in simple things, your total life changes. Your mind changes, and positivity enters your life. You leave behind all the baggage that has held you back. Being grateful and graceful leads to happiness and helps you find your purpose.

The emotion of gratitude enables us to notice the good things in our lives and to value and be grateful for them. It is a way of identifying the good without taking it for granted. When we experience gratitude, we become more open to receiving and sharing positive energy with those around us.

Gratitude is a state of mind that allows us to connect more with our environment and focus on the present moment. It helps us to stop dwelling on the past and worrying about the future. Being grateful for what we have in life helps us to become more thankful for the gifts given to us as they come.

I can do differently expressing gratitude, like taking time during meditation to reflect on the things we're grateful for, or writing a heartfelt thank you note for someone essential. (We have lost this art of writing, which we need to do more of.) Practicing gratitude helps us to recognize the abundance in our lives and to develop a stronger connection with ourselves and others.

Gratitude is also a great tool to help us stay focused on our goals and appreciate our progress in life. Acknowledging our achievements and successes is a great way to stay positive and motivated. Think of this as praise you receive at work or school, or as a compliment. Without having an ego, feel the love of being acknowledged.

If we express gratitude, it can significantly aid in discovering happiness and satisfaction in our daily lives. By expressing gratitude, we redirect our attention from what we may lack to what we already possess. To be present now helps us notice the grace in our lives.

Recognizing and appreciating the good things in our lives can help us to manifest our dreams and goals. Gratitude encourages us to take risks, to be creative, and to act toward our desired outcomes.

Expressing gratitude can aid in cultivating a more positive outlook on life. When we practice gratitude, we become more resilient and better cope with life's difficulties. It also allows us to enjoy life's small pleasures and savor the moments that bring us joy.

When I lived in Rhode Island there was a law that stated you could not leave your car overnight on the street in Providence. I was suing the property owner next to me because of an easement. An easement gives another person the right to access or use someone else's property. I found out the previous owner owned both properties and removed the wall between the two properties. The owner did not include in the sale of both homes an easement. I lost and had to pay a monthly fee to the owner for 6 feet. I could not pass this fee to my tenant then, as it would be unfair.

One day while driving home, I had a moment where I cried so hard that I couldn't catch my breath. I remember crying and praying. I repeatedly asserted it was not fair. It exhausted me despite doing everything by the book, and I worried about how I could pay for this. To cover the cost, I took on a second job at a shoe department store.

I remember one Saturday, my pockets were empty because I had paid off all my bills. I went to work that evening and sold a pair of shoes. The customer was so happy that he found the shoes he had been searching for as a Christmas gift that he gave me $10; the next customer was even more pleased and gave me $20. I could not believe the luck I had. I was so happy because I had no money and could not afford to eat.

I drove to Wendy's and placed my order, and something happened when I went to the drive-through window to pay. The worker said, "*Your food is free. Thank God for this day and for what you received today.*" And I tell you, I had goosebumps all over my arms. I said, "*Thank you,*" and drove home, crying all the way. God blessed me with **GRACE**.

When I tell you to manifest, or use your intuition, or ground yourself, or change from within, these things raise your vibrations. We all have these capabilities within ourselves. Be grateful for what you have. Every morning, as soon as I wake up, I say, "*Thank you, God, for all the blessings coming my way,*".

We've all had moments that hit hard and we all go through difficulties. It is how we look at the overall issue that affects us. You can look at it continuously, saying that everything is always challenging. **STOP IT!** Do not call hardness to yourself. Instead, repeat, *"Everything is easy for me, as I am tougher than the storm."* Every problem or obstacle always has a solution. It is how you see it, process it, plan and set a goal to see you through it. I have decided to always look for a bright side to everything. Once I did this, my life changed. I no longer fret over the small things—even the big stuff, as it will eventually resolve. We do not need to give it power. Why are you letting it take from your peace? It is hard, but you are resilient and will come out through it.

Gratitude is an active practice that can help align us with our true purpose in life. It's about acknowledging the often-overlooked blessings and embracing them wholeheartedly.

This journey reminds us that gratitude is a transformative force. It empowers us to find the silver lining even in the darkest clouds and cultivates a resilient spirit.

With gratitude, challenges become stepping stones, and those moments of grace shine through. Don't forget that gratitude is a powerful tool that can improve your life and enlighten your journey.

SHINE SO BRIGHT YOU BLIND THEM!

GRATEFUL FOR ALL THE BLESSINGS COMING MY WAY!

I HAVE AN ABUNDANCE OF MONEY, HEALTH, AND SUCCESS!

WHEN EVERY THING IS FALLING INTO PLACE, REMEMBER TO SAY THANK YOU!

Chapter Two

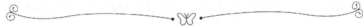

What is Manifesting?

Manifesting is creating what you want by using your thoughts, beliefs, and energy. The concept is that your thoughts and choices can shape your reality. You can create positive change and attract desired outcomes by aligning your mindset, emotions, and actions. Manifesting involves tapping into the universal energy and harnessing it to bring your dreams to fruition.

Remember to add your intentions when you manifest. When you set intentions, you state what you want to achieve through your actions. It is the reason you are manifesting what you desire. It is as simple as saying, "*I am thankful for our new home. My family and I no longer must live in a shelter and can enjoy a new roof over our heads.*" It is essential to establish your intentions for anything you manifest, and you'll want to set them before any big event that you are undertaking.

When manifesting your desires into your everyday routine can produce extraordinary advantages. It allows you to shift your mindset from a passive approach to an empowered one, where you actively take part in creating the life you desire. Your thoughts and actions can become more intentional and self-aware through manifesting practice. It fosters determination and resilience by cultivating a positive outlook on life.

If you make manifesting a part of your daily routine, you can improve your self-awareness and focus, and achieve your goals. Try it, you have nothing to lose but so much to gain, like peace of mind, love, and an understanding that you can take to heart.

It is crucial to understand your goals clearly. By that, I mean having a clear sign of what you want or what you need. You do not need many things that are frivolous and ego-centered. Take, for example, a $1000 handbag or $500 sneakers. Is that a want or a need? Reflect on what you truly desire and use "I AM" and "I HAVE" statements to define your aspirations. Ask yourself: "*Who am I becoming?*" and "*What do I want to have in my life?*"

Take a piece of paper and write what you would like to manifest using the "I AM, and I HAVE" manifestations. For example, *"I am successful in business. I have offers for collaborations to skyrocket my business and earnings."* Acknowledge their power by speaking affirmations aloud. This process solidifies your intentions and sets the foundation for manifestation, as your words have power.

Visualization is another key and powerful tool in manifesting. I want you to sit in a comfortable chair or sofa, which makes your body feel relaxed. Now close your eyes, and take three deep breaths. Do this three times more. Once you feel your body is fully relaxed, get your imagination juices flowing. I want you to create a vivid mental image of something that you have manifested. See yourself signing that contract for that new business endeavor, or getting that acceptance that you are closing on your new home. Feel the happiness this brings to you. That feeling is the energy that will attract what you manifest because you are at that vibrational level. Your manifestation reflects what you put out, and it aligns with your state of mind.

Engage your senses, too. Say you want to get a new car, use your imagination to smell the scent of a new car, hear its horn, and how you would look sitting inside the car driving it. This is what it means when you visually see yourself as if you have already manifested your goals. Immerse yourself in this experience and allow yourself to feel the emotions associated with your achievements. Visualization helps you align your energy and focus with your desired reality. For some, visualizing something that is not there is hard. I used to print an image of what I wanted and hang it in front of me. I would use a picture of a beautiful office desk setting for a new job I was manifesting for myself. Therefore, I created a mental picture to manifest that new job, apartment or home, and luck.

Reflect on your current beliefs, thoughts, and emotions. Are they supporting or hindering your manifestations? Identify any limiting beliefs or doubts that may hold you back. Replace negative self-talk with positive affirmations and affirm your confidence in manifesting your dreams. Cultivating a positive and empowered mindset is essential for successful manifestation.

Manifesting is not just about dreaming; it requires taking inspired action. To achieve your goals, it's best to identify practical steps that can bring you closer to them. Break these steps into manageable tasks and create an action plan. Seize opportunities that align with your aspirations and remain open to new possibilities. Taking consistent and intentional action reinforces your commitment to manifest and propels you forward.

Trust that the universe has a plan for you and that your manifestations are coming. There are some manifestations that will take longer than others. Let go of attachment to specific outcomes and surrender to the divine timing. Have faith that what you desire is already in the process of manifesting. Think LAW OF ATTRACTION! Trust that everything is unfolding as it should and be patient and resilient on your journey. Trusting the process and letting go of control allows the universe to work magic in bringing your desires to life.

Many people will tell you that manifesting doesn't work. Ask if they have tried manifesting. It will surprise you how many people speak about something they know nothing about. Remember, *"Do not let them dim your light. Shine so bright it blinds them."*

Manifesting enhances focus and helps achieve aspirations. You can manifest having friends, a new job, a new place to live and more. Say this aloud if you want to have friends: *"I am manifesting friends that can mentor me, are not ego-driven, and have good intentions and a good heart, so that we can help one another rise."*

Now repeat this for one for a new job: *"I am manifesting an employment that will treat me well with benefits and salary. This employment has an amazing retirement plan and four weeks of paid time off. My new co-workers are a family, and we get along beautifully. I have signed my new employment contract and will start on Monday."*

Say this one for a new place to live, *"I have signed my new lease or new home closing contract. I have the keys in my hand, and I am turning the knob and walking into my new home."*

You can change it up to suit your needs. You can say it daily or twice a week. It is all up to you how many times you want to say your manifestations. Remember, what you say has power.

Manifesting is not just about dreaming; it requires taking inspired action. Explore practical measures that can help you make progress toward your desired outcomes. Remember, when you manifest, you call that into being. Depending on what you are trying to manifest, you need to put in the work to make it happen. For example, you are manifesting wanting to win the lottery. You cannot just expect to win if you do not play. Go down to the store to purchase a ticket. If you do not go to the store, how do you expect to win?

Dividing tasks into smaller, more manageable components gets you closer to your goal. A well-planned strategy is crucial to stay focused and achieve your intentions. Seize opportunities that align with your aspirations and remain open to new possibilities. You show your unwavering commitment to achieving your goals by consistently and intentionally acting. This approach propels you forward and brings you closer to realizing your dreams.

I manifested getting employment within a law firm as a legal secretary. Online I found a cute office setting picture with a decorated desk. I put it up on the wall of my bedroom, so it was the first thing I saw each morning. I said out loud, *"I have accepted the new job offer as a legal secretary. The employment is close to home and the office staff is amazing and treats me as a part of the team. All my co-workers get along with me and I get two weeks of paid time off with benefits and a retirement plan."*

I next applied to newspaper ads for the position I was seeking. I spoke to friends and family to ask if they had heard of any job that was hiring. Companies may share opportunities through word-of-mouth before posting online. Each time I went to an interview, I repeated, *"God, give me the words to say. Make my words appealing to get hired."* After my interviews, I took a moment to give thanks. I was hired and worked at the law firm until I remarried and moved back to New York.

Trust that the universe has a plan for you and that your manifestations are coming. Let go of attachment to specific outcomes and surrender to the divine timing. Have faith that what you desire is already in the process of manifesting. Be patient and resilient during the manifestation journey, knowing that things are happening as they should. Trusting the process and letting go of control, allow the universe to work magic in bringing your desires to materialize.

NOTHING IS EVER A COINCIDENCE, IT WAS MEANT TO BE!

MANIFEST ALL THE GOALS YOU WANT TO ACHIEVE.

SUCCESS ABUNDANCE & PROSPERITY KNOCK ON MY DOOR ALL THE TIME.

WHEN YOU ARE AT THE SAME LEVEL OF WHAT YOU MANIFEST THE UNIVERSE MAKES IT HAPPEN!

Chapter Three

What is Intuition?

Intuition is to know something with no proof or evidence. It's a powerful tool that can guide us through life by helping us make better decisions and tap into our spiritual guidance. Our inner knowing can make us aware of potential dangers, direct us to an opportune time, or give us insight into a situation.

Your angels and spiritual guides communicate with you all the time. The way you perceive them depends on you. It can be something subtle, like an idea that pops into your head, or an inner voice that can guide you to decisions based on your wisdom. Intuition is a sixth sense, a heightened awareness of our surroundings that comes from within. We can use intuition in our personal lives, our relationships, and our work. My angels and guides gave me the idea for a podcast to inspire and help people. We may receive intuitive messages through dreams, visions, and gut feelings. These messages can help us decide our spiritual paths and connect with our higher selves.

When we use intuition, we tap into a source with infinite potential. Our intuition is a powerful tool to access information beyond the physical realm. The details can provide guidance and insight from your higher self, angels, spirit guides, or the Universe.

Before we can access our intuition, we need to create an environment. A way to honor our connection with our intuition is through gratitude. Expressing gratitude opens the space for us to access our intuitive guidance. We can also use our imagination to tap into our intuition. Our imagination is a powerful tool. When we imagine something and permit ourselves to be creative, we can create powerful shifts and changes in our lives.

Here's a practice to help you tap into your intuition. Get a notebook to script your thoughts, goals, and what you're currently manifesting. Scripting involves writing your desires as though they have already happened. Once you have finished writing, say it out loud. This creates a space for your intuition to emerge. The law of attraction states that you attract what you say. Keep a notebook next to you so you can write it all down. It can be a dream, a vision, or a memory that pops out of nowhere. By trusting your intuition, you can invite positive changes and progress into your life.

Has someone ever invited you to go out with friends on a Friday night, but felt it was better to stay in? You later turn on the news and see a fire or gunshots at the location where you would have gone. This exemplifies how intuition, backed by your angels and spiritual guides, can help us avoid potential harm.

Intuition can also help us in relationships. We may sense when someone is being unfaithful, untruthful, or unsupportive. We may even feel when it's time to move on from a relationship. Let them go, as they were only supposed to be beside you for a time. You learned the lesson you needed from this person. It is time to move on. Yes, you will be sad, but as I mentioned, there is always a bright side. This is being removed for the new relationship to come to you. You may even feel when it is time to take a chance and open ourselves up to a deeper connection. Though this sometimes comes when you least expect it, do not be afraid to love. Open your heart and remove the fear. Fear needs to leave for the love to overflow.

If she or he left and took all their belongings, and you wonder how you will pay the rent, manifest finding a roommate. *"I have found the perfect roommate that is caring, helpful, and pays their rent on time and is clean. We both get along with each other and have many things in common."* If you are not looking for a roommate, look at your finances and plan how much you can afford and move to another less expensive apartment. I love moving. It means a new chapter is opening, and I am shedding the old. Looking at the bright side of things is my motto. Out with the old and in with the new.

In the workplace, intuition can help us determine the best action in difficult situations. We may know when it is the right time to ask for a promotion or when to look for another job. Intuition can also help us discern whether we should trust someone with our business. When you tell someone about your plans, they could try to steal your ideas. I created a podcast episode about the benefits of keeping your plans to yourself until you achieve them.

Here are the five key reasons it is beneficial:

1. Maintain Focus and Avoid Distractions

Sharing your goals can sometimes invite unwanted opinions and distractions. By keeping your plans private, you can maintain focus and avoid being swayed by others' doubts or suggestions. This allows you to stay true to your vision and decide based on your convictions.

2. Protecting Your Dreams from Negativity

Only some people will understand and support your dreams. If you share your plans too soon, people might react negatively or discourage you, even if they mean well. Shielding your goals from criticism until you achieve them helps them to flourish positively.

3. Avoiding the Pressure of Expectations

When you announce your plans to the world, you might feel pressured to meet certain expectations, which can be overwhelming. Privacy can help you work at your own pace and avoid the burden of others' expectations until you succeed.

4. Maintaining a Sense of Mystery

There's something magical about unveiling your achievements when no one saw them coming. Keeping your plans under wrap creates an air of mystery and intrigue. This allows you to surprise others and yourself with your accomplishments.

5. Protection from Over-sharing

It's essential to be mindful of what you share on social media. It's tempting to showcase every step of our journey, but doing so can have downsides. If you post your vacation picks of the airport, hotel, etc., on social media, you are over-sharing. You're not in a competition to outdo others. Over-sharing can lead to a sense of superficial accomplishment and may even invite envy or unnecessary judgment. Celebrating your achievements is excellent. Posting your new job with a pay rate is ego-based and unnecessary.

Intuition can also gain insight into our spiritual growth. We may receive intuitive messages through dreams, visions, and gut feelings. These messages can help us decide our spiritual paths and connect with our higher selves. The key to understanding and using intuition is to become more aware of our inner voice. This requires us to be more mindful of our thoughts and feelings.

We must be open to our intuition and listen to its guidance. Take the writing of this book, for example. I did not tell anyone I was writing it. I did not want to get discouraged and just stop. But I knew that if this could help one person, I had to keep this gift quiet and surprise people once I completed it.

We can plan the future, but we must live in the present. We all worry about many things. When I was pregnant with my son, I was wondering how I would pay my rent. Note my ex-husband was not working, and I made excuses for it. (But that is another story. Ergo, the reason it says ex.) I created a plan to save extra money and stopped ordering fast food. I saved up a month of rent, and though I was able to pay the next month's rent, I wasn't able to pay for anything else. I ran out of baby formula for my son. Well, you can imagine I was beside myself. I sat down, took three deep breaths, and asked for guidance, and I heard a voice that said, "*Contact the place where you did the baby classes.*"

OMG! I had forgotten I was told I could contact them if I needed formula and diapers. I rushed to dial the number. That same day, they gave me a can of baby formula and diapers. This was a godsend! Trust your intuition, as it will not lead you wrong. There are many ways to tune into our intuition. We can practice meditation to become more mindful and aware of our inner voice. We can also create sacred space and ask our angels and spirit guides for guidance, as I did when I sat down and took those three breaths.

Our intuition is a powerful tool for deciding and navigating our lives. By tuning into our intuition, we can gain greater insight into our lives and embrace our spiritual guidance. Our intuition is an asset that can help us make the best decisions and achieve greater fulfillment.

I will leave you with this quote from Author Adil Ahmed: *"Just because you don't share it on social media doesn't mean you are not up to big things. Live it and stay low-key. Privacy is everything."*

WHAT IS MEANT FOR YOU, WILL BE FOR YOU AND CAN NOT BE TAKEN AWAY.

RAISE YOUR VIBRATIONS TO MEET YOUR MANIFESTATIONS.

PEOPLE LOVE MY WORK AND CAN NOT GET ENOUGH OF IT.

WHEN GRACE KNOCKS ON YOUR DOOR WATCH FOR ALL THE BLESSINGS AND CHANGES IN YOUR LIFE.

Chapter Four

Do You Know Your Words Have Power?

Your words hold an immense power. They shape your reality and influence your thoughts, beliefs, and actions. With the right words, we can tap into tremendous power and create positive changes in our lives and the world.

How can you harness the power of your words to create positive change? By using positive affirmations, you can reprogram your mind and align your thoughts with your desires. The key is choosing words that empower, inspire, and uplift you. We can cultivate positive energy and call positivity into our lives by repeating positive affirmations. We can use affirmations to remind ourselves of our strengths and to build self-confidence.

How you use them is very important because when you say positive things, you attract positive things. When you say negative things, that's what you will attract.

Bullies use hurtful words, and it causes devastating effects on adults and children's well-being and self-esteem. They can be as simple as *"You're stupid; You can't do that;* or *No one loves you."* Using these terms makes you feel worthless and lowers your vibrational energy. Positive affirmation helps adults and children build resilience and strengthens their self-esteem.

By repeating affirmations daily, you can strengthen your self-worth and inner strength. This can reprogram your subconscious mind. With this process, you can develop a positive mindset, overcome negativity, and regain your confidence. Positive affirmations can boost your self-esteem and help you stand up to bullying. Make it a non-negotiable aspect of your daily practice, and you'll see its positive impact on your confidence. Make it a priority to affirm yourself daily and watch how your mindset shifts towards positivity and self-assurance. Remember, you can control how you feel about yourself, and positive affirmations are a powerful tool to help you do just that.

I saw a science experiment once that involved two beautiful roses. One rose received constant streams of positive, loving words while the other, received negative, harmful remarks. As the experiment unfolded, the incredible powers of words and action was shown. The rose exposed to negativity withered away while the one nurtured by positivity thrived.

We must be mindful and intentional when speaking, especially in the presence of children. Even when we do not think they are listening, they listen to every word we say. They're like sponges, internalizing the messages that they hear. We must realize the impact our terms can have on children and adults alike. You must be mindful of your speech and foster a positive, uplifting environment. We must create a nurturing space for growth and development.

Remember, kids pick up gestures, too. You do not want your child to mimic you doing the wrong thing. It is better for them to imitate you singing a positive message to yourself than berating yourself for forgetting to do something one time.

Now, here are three tips for effectively using positive affirmations:

- Be specific and present using positive language. For example, "*I am a guiding light of love and healing.*" Say it out loud. You harness the power of your words and send your intentions to the universe and the law of attraction invites them to bring your desires to completion.

- Two, repeat them with conviction. Repeat your affirmations multiple times daily and say them confidently and firmly. Bottom line, believe what you say. Feel it with every fiber of your being.

- As you recite your affirmations, feel positive emotions, and connect with the positive feelings related to your goal. Visualize and feel the joy, gratitude, and confidence from achieving your goals.

Your angels and guides want you to know the power your words hold. They encourage you to choose words that uplift and inspire yourself and others. Why is it important to choose words of positivity and avoid negative self-talk? This is simple, as negative self-talk and terms of limitations hinder your growth and manifestations. You can change your mindset by using positive affirmations to transform your life. We align ourselves with the vibration of abundance, attract positive experiences, and create a life of purpose and fulfillment.

I bet some of you have said in your lifetime, *"Oh, I never have enough money! John is so lucky. He has won four scratch-off tickets"* or *"Jane gets anything she wants, and I never do."*

Stop calling this negativity into your life. Instead, say, *"My bank account is overflowing"*, or *"I have attracted luck and prosperity into my life."* The mind uses your voice and creates a picture with your words. If you repeat not having enough, you will call it to yourself. **Please stop!** I am going to repeat myself. Stop repeating those words and say instead, *"I have health and healing in my life. I am growing with love, luck, and a mindful heart with gratitude. I have abundance and prosperity knocking at my door."* Change your conscious mindset.

I remember when my son was younger. He was told by another student that he was bad at soccer. He came to me crying. It hurt to see my son down. I told him to say that he was an excellent soccer player, and that sometimes people say things without knowing. I told him that the next time he was told that, he should respond with, *"That is your opinion and not anyone else's"*. It is important to remind children to speak up and not be silent. My son knew he was good, and that was all that mattered. Children do not understand that what they say can hurt others, even if that was not the intention.

When you shift your consciousness from a perspective of lack, where you believe there is limited abundance, to one of abundance, you have reached a new level. You call positivity into your life, which will shift your energy.

Another way to use the power of words is to recognize your potential and the potential of those around you. Our terms can help establish a community and promote interconnectedness. Using your words can inspire and affirm the capabilities of others. We can use our terms to create space to provide others' safety and acceptance.

We can also use words to spread awareness and create social change. Speaking up for what you believe in draws attention to important issues, and questioning traditions can lead to a fairer society.

Finally, we can use our words to be mindful of our environment. By choosing words such as "sustainability" and "earth-friendly," we can emphasize the importance of protecting our planet.

Your words have tremendous power, and by using them more intentionally, you can create a positive shift in your life. Words have the power to focus on abundance, recognize potential, and create positive change in society. By understanding the power of your words, we can use them to create a brighter, more hopeful future.

YOUR WORDS HAVE POWER!

TAKE THE TIME TO SEE ALL THE SURROUNDING BEAUTY! WHEN YOU RUSH, YOU MISS OUT ON THE VIEW.

POSITIVE THOUGHTS LEAD TO BLESSINGS FROM THE DIVINE!

GRATITUDE ATTRACTS LOVE!

Chapter Five

How to Change from Within?

The first step in changing from within is to have self-love. This begins with understanding your own worth and developing an appreciation for yourself. To transform yourself, you must believe in your power and learn to love yourself. Once you realize your capabilities, you can take the steps to create the desired changes.

We must first understand ourselves and our feelings and emotions to change. That means knowing our thoughts, feelings, and beliefs about ourselves and how they affect our lives. Understanding our personal values and goals can point out areas for improvement and the steps to take. Recognizing patterns that hinder change then becomes easier.

As I mentioned, I have an ex-husband. When I was doing his immigration paperwork to bring him to this country, my therapist asked, *"Does he speak English? or What job will he get once he is in the USA?"* I replied that I was taking it one step at a time, the first being getting him here. Like I said before, I was in therapy and was getting information that an outsider was seeing something I didn't. So I began having conversations with him about how he could learn English or what he would do for a living once he got to New York. He always said learning cost too much money, or that I wouldn't be involved in what he did when he got to New York, so don't ask. You get where I am going with this. I refused to acknowledge what others were seeing, and I could not see what they saw. All the red flags were present, but I was blinded. After the birth of my son, my eyes opened, and I divorced him.

We have all, at one time or another, ignored the signs being sent to us. Let me tell you this: There were many, many signs that I did not want to see. They denied the case for his paperwork for immigration. He would tell me things that just didn't make sense. All things to that would make you question yourself. In the end, I changed for myself because I wanted better. A person who could help me with baby formula, a person who did not expected me to send him money when I did not have money coming in. A person who valued me.

I am a resilient woman, as many are. We keep moving forward without looking back. I set many goals for my family and myself. I work towards them to manifest them into reality. The most important thing is you must change for yourself and **NOT FOR ANYONE ELSE**.

When embarking on the self-change journey, we must be kind to ourselves. We must learn to practice self-care, showing ourselves the kindness and support we would give our friends and loved ones. Positive self-talk is essential in improving our self-esteem and allowing us to believe in ourselves and our abilities. We can take care of our physical and mental health by exercising regularly, eating healthy, and getting enough sleep. It's essential to handle stress and anxiety. Some good options include seeking professional help, confiding in someone you trust, writing in a journal, or doing things you enjoy. These strategies can help you cope with your feelings.

One great way to begin self-reflection is to look at your current relationships and how they affect you. Ask yourself if your partner or spouse is supportive of you and if not, what are the reasons? You might be stuck in a pattern of breaking up and getting back together with someone who cheats or does something wrong. **STOP** the sequence, and do not allow yourself to be taken advantage of. Establishing connections that promote your personal growth and highlight your best qualities is crucial. It is essential to recognize when your relationships are unhealthy and to take action to make changes.

As I stated, I recognized that my marriage was one-sided. I gave more than I received. This realization helped me end that cycle. I moved on, not knowing what was to come. I like the term, "When you least expect it." Because this was exactly how I met my husband now. I was not dating and was afraid because I had a baby and had to be careful whom I brought into his life and mine. I had to not fear the unknown, as that stops most people from finding the one.

An important part of any change within yourself is to ensure you are setting boundaries in your life. This means you must be able to say "No" to situations that do not bring you happiness. This can be hard to do, mainly if you are used to being taken advantage of, but it is essential to move forward and make changes. Once you say "No," it gets effortless, and you will wonder why you hadn't used it sooner.

Once we have taken the time to understand ourselves better, it is crucial to be honest and open with ourselves about the changes we want to make. This includes identifying our goals, dreams, and aspirations and understanding what steps must be taken to achieve them. It is essential to be realistic about the changes we want and be willing to take action to make them happen. Also, it is necessary to remember that change is a process that takes time. We must be patient and consistent with our efforts to create lasting changes.

Another great way to make these changes is to ensure you take the time to do things for yourself. For women, this could be practicing yoga, getting your hair and nails done, or going for walks for thought in nature. For men, this can be to freshen up by visiting the barbershop, exercising, or spending time with friends. These activities can effectively reduce stress levels while providing self-reflection and self-discovery. Taking a break from your everyday life and being in the moment is a great way to help yourself move forward and find gratitude.

Synchronicity can be a potent method to establish a connection with your intuition and inner self. It is when you notice a pattern or message that initially seems unrelated, but then reveals its true meaning. Synchronicity can mean you're on the right path and getting guidance from the Universe.

Becoming more aware of synchronicities can help us connect to our intuition and get simple answers about our choices. When faced with a dilemma or decision, pay attention to what happens around you for confirmation that you're heading in the right direction. Pay attention to repeating numbers, coincidences, and meaningful conversations. For example, seeing the time 11:11. This angelic number has many meanings. I believe it means that change is coming, and I am aligned with my angels.

Synchronicity is also a reminder that life is magical. There is so much more available to us than meets the eye–if we open to it! When synchronicities reveal themselves, take time to pause and appreciate their beauty. Connect with gratitude for all that life has given you, and note what it could mean for your future.

Synchronicities can also be signs from your angels or spirit guides, telling you that everything is unfolding as it should be. Messages can come in different forms, like dreams, symbols, or physical sensations. They may have a connection to the chakras, which are energy centers in the body. Noting these brief hints will help connect you with your intuition and give clarity about hard decisions. For a time now, I have been seeing and finding white feathers everywhere. There are many meanings to this. I deeply believe that this symbol represents my guardian angels and holds a profound significance for me. When I'm in need of guidance, I find them, or if I asked a question and requested a sign, I discovered it.

You can tap into the power of synchronicity by being more mindful of daily events, especially those that catch your attention or stir up different emotions. Pay attention to repeating numbers, patterns in your life, sudden meetings, and dreams. You may also wonder if there is a reason it attracted you to certain people, places, and situations. Trust your inner guidance and look for the symbolic meaning in the most mundane experiences. You can appreciate the synchronicities already there. Be sure to take a moment to write these occurrences, share them with friends, and note their sheer brilliance. You will experience pleasant surprises as synchronicity manifests in your life.

Finally, understand that self-care and synchronicities are the foundation of any inner transformation. Only when you take a step back to nurture yourself, listen to your heart, and understand how life's natural patterns can shape your journey will you be able to make lasting changes within yourself. Set reasonable goals that will ultimately lead to meaningful life changes. Take positive action to make those changes happen. But above all else, always remember to practice self-care and kindness towards yourself and those around you!

Embrace meaningful relationships where possible, and surround yourself with positive influences who will lift you up and support your growth. Hit up that friend who keeps asking you out to just talk. Your real friends will want to spend time with you. Do not seek those who will not respond to your text or calls. Let them move on. Find better friends that will truly support you and help you rise. The more invested you become in improving yourself from within, the more rewarding your actual inner change will be.

VIBRATE AT THE FREQUENCY YOU WISH TO MANIFEST!

LET GO OF THE OLD TO ALLOW THE NEW TO COME IN!

FEAR NOTHING. RISE ABOVE IT!

WHAT YOU MANIFEST APPEARS WHEN YOU LEAST EXPECT IT!

Chapter Six

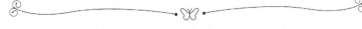

What is Grounding?

Grounding is a technique that involves connecting the body to the Earth's surface by walking barefoot on grass, soil, or water. It is balancing the spiritual, mental, and physical energies within your body, similar to how you balance your chakras. Regular grounding can reduce stress, anxiety, and depression by harmonizing your body, mind, and spirit with the world around you.

Grounding is best done by taking time to connect with yourself and with nature. This can include activities like taking a walk-through nature, or simply sitting in a quiet space outdoors with your feet on the grass or in water. During this time, take a few moments to close your eyes and take a few deep breaths. Visualize your energy connecting with the Earth's energy and the energy of the surrounding environment. Imagine your feet as roots digging themselves to the ground. Feel the energy of the Earth beneath your feet, the surrounding air, and the sun above. Allow yourself to become one with the environment. Remember to say your intentions when you ground yourself.

When grounding, it can also be helpful to focus on your breath and direct your attention to your body and the sensations it is experiencing. Focus on your feet and how they connect with the ground. Feel the energy that is being exchanged between you and the Earth. Allow yourself to feel grounded and connected to the world around you.

Grounding can be a powerful aid for healing and emotional balance. When practiced regularly, it can help to reduce stress and anxiety, improve mental clarity, and help to create a sense of peace and well-being. It can also help to open the body and release any negative energy that has become stuck.

You can easily practice grounding anytime and anywhere, making it a simple yet powerful technique. Set aside a few moments each day to connect with your environment and yourself. Take three deep breaths and allow yourself to relax and let go of any worries or concerns. Feel the connection between your body and the ground and allow yourself to be nourished by the energy of the Earth.

The first time you try it, you might feel silly or awkward, but do not let this stop you from continuing to do it every day. Make it a part of your morning routine, along with stretching or exercising, getting ready for work, or sitting down to breakfast. The best thing about grounding is that you can do it literally wherever you are. You can take three deep breaths and release any stress that you may have in a matter of minutes. You will notice how much more relaxed you become after just a few times. The warmth of the sun, and the coolness of fresh air all surround you like an embrace.

I went early one morning to the park to ground myself. I took five sticks of selenite with me. Selenite is a crystal that promotes peace, mental clarity, calm, and well-being. I went to a grassy area and sat on the ground with my bare feet. Placing one selenite stick in front of me, two on either side and one behind, I faced the sun. I vocalized my intentions during my prayer. Setting intentions can bring positivity, happiness, and balance to your life. Crystals can enhance this energy and help you manifest your intentions more effectively. Whenever you are using crystals, set your intentions. I took the stick and cleansed myself with it, to remove the negative energy and ground me. You can say, *"Thank you for the beauty of nature surrounding me."* Look to the sun and manifest your goals as if you have already received them. When you are done, rise and go on your way. You will feel the energy in you being connected to the one source and your higher self.

After I did this, I stood up and saw clovers in the grass. I thought, wouldn't it be funny if I found a four-leaf clover? Upon searching, I found one. It was that fast. I had it laminated, and I carry it with me in my wallet for good luck. Note you can also do this in the water. I enjoy going to the beach and walking around in the ocean. It feels so good and relaxing.

When you take the time each day to do something for yourself, you will feel it. You can analyze things differently. Time spent grounding will help you start your day off right, helping you become more centered so that you can make wise decisions when needed. Please let me know how you feel after grounding yourself.

WHAT YOU ARE LOOKING FOR IS SEARCHING FOR YOU! PAY ATTENTION TO SYNCHRONCITY!

DO NOT CLOSE YOURSELF OFF TO FEAR. FACE IT HEAD ON FOR CHANGE TO HAPPEN!

THE DIVINE LIGHT IS ON THE OTHER SIDE, OPEN THE DOOR TO ALLOW IT IN!

WHEN IDEAS & CREATIVITY HITS YOU SAY, THANK YOU, AS THE DIVINE IS AT WORK!

Chapter Seven

How is Meditation Helpful?

We can use meditation to access our intuition. Meditation is a great way to clear our minds and be open to the messages from our intuition. Through meditation, we can slow down and be present in the moment.

If you are feeling stressed and depressed, meditation can be a powerful aid to help ground you. So, take some time out of your day - even if it's just five to twenty minutes - and find a peaceful place for yourself. Put away your cell phone and ignore those emails that are clamoring for your attention! Sit down, close your eyes, and take three deep breaths in through your mouth and letting it out slowly. Let go of any tension that's been building up, so your body can be at ease. You'll find that when you meditate daily, you feel recharged and connected with your higher self. If you have a problem, use this practice to tap into your intuition and get simple answers.

As we deepen our meditation practice, we become more aware of the messages from our angels and spiritual guides. There are several ways that you can meditate.

Here are some that you can find and follow on YouTube:
- Guided meditation video with soft music.
- Video with soft music and/or white noise with no guided talk.
- A black background with no music or talking.

The beginning is always hard as you sit and are not sure what to do. Now, I would like you to sit with your hands on your lap, either face up or palms down. Take three deep breaths through your nose and out your mouth. You will repeat the breathing three more times. Let your entire body relax, starting with your shoulders, then hands, and lastly your legs. You will feel a sense of bliss and relaxation you probably never felt before. It will feel good, and you will want to repeat it many times.

When I meditated, it was difficult for me at first. My body could not relax. But I kept doing it. I searched on YouTube for many videos to help me. I love the guided meditations as someone speaks to you in a low voice and tells you to take deep breaths. Next, they say to let your shoulders drop to release the stress you are carrying. Then, it goes back to the breath. Know that your mind will want to wander. Keep calling it back to center yourself. It is alright if your thoughts race. Your mind is so focused on breathing and relaxing that different things will pop up in your mind. You might get so relaxed that you fall asleep. This has happened to me many times, and it feels so good. I will not force myself to stay awake. I just let it be. The first time I fully relaxed my body, it felt as if I was lightweight and flying. It felt so amazing. Everyone experiences meditation in different ways. I am sharing my own experiences while practicing it. Now you do not have to meditate for long periods of time. Just sit for five minutes or ten minutes if you can. You will unwind and a calmness will take over you like you have never fathomed before.

Now that you have awakened a new mind, body, and spirit within you, clarity to see things from new perspectives will become second nature for you. Once you start your meditative journey, you will wonder why you never started before. While you are meditating, you can ask your angels and guides questions. You will get the answers you seek. Trust your gut and you'll find solutions to any issues that arise. It is slow at first, but once you practice, it comes easily. That sense of knowing grows each day. As you develop, meditation will help guide you along this fresh path of enlightenment.

WE ARE LIKE CATERPILLARS GOING THROUGH LIFE & GROW INTO BEAUTIFUL BUTTERFLIES, WE ARE DESTINED TO BE!

TRANSFORM YOURSELF INTO YOUR OWN BUTTERFLY & SHINE!

OPEN YOUR HEART TO LOVE AND REMOVE THE FEAR FOR IT TO COME IN!

CLOSE DOORS THAT NO LONGER SERVE YOU!

Chapter Eight

Finding Happiness

Take everything that you have absorbed from this book and strive to attain its deep knowledge and understanding. Transform yourself and speak up. Do not stay quiet any longer. Make sure no one takes advantage of you. Be happy with yourself for your life to change. Take those moments that will give you the laughter you need by hanging out with your friends. Take risks if you want to do something, or you will wonder what if?

You must journey into the depths of your soul and decide what is worth fighting for. Have the courage to change your life that reflects your happiness - from the quality of your relationships to the career you choose.

Once I started thinking of myself, I changed to be who I am now. Yes, I evolved into a better me for myself and not for others—a woman who loves her family, job, and friends. However, I also learned that I could say no. The newfound person you see has grown over the years. They say as you age you become more insightful. I must agree with that.

Become aware and grateful for what you have in your life - from the roof over your head to the food on the table. Appreciate what you have and express your gratitude each day. Work on developing a positive relationship with yourself. Loving yourself is essential to loving the other relationships you will have and sets the tone for future relationships.

Focus on manifesting your goals. Use your intuition to guide you and believe in yourself, even when you cannot see the outcome. Believe that you can achieve anything and that everything is possible. Your words have power, so use them wisely. Fulfillment is within your reach. Believe in yourself.

Visualize your dreams and think about what it would feel like to achieve them. Feel the emotions that it generates to break the surface. Tear down the barrier you had to put up for yourself and allow that love to come through. Seek experiences that make you happy and delight in them. Practice self-care by making time for your passions, your hobbies, and your interests.

Enjoy the little things in life, like fresh flowers, a good book, a great coffee, or a beautiful sunset. Change yourself from within. Let go of old unhealthy baggage and beliefs that no longer serve you. Get to know the new you better, your emotions, and your new passions. What do you want at this stage in your life? Seek the answers to pinpoint what it means to you now. Spend time with people who bring out the best in you. Surround yourself with people who lift you and make you feel good. Cut out toxic relationships and situations from your life that discourage you.

Finding happiness is possible. It takes some reflection to see things in a new light, to overcome many obstacles, but in the end, your angels and spiritual guides are with you. Take the time to reflect on what makes you happy and do not be afraid to change your life to pursue those things. Believe in yourself and in what you can achieve. Remember, you have infinite potential, and the limitations are those that you put on yourself. Do not limit yourself. Using your intuition to manifest your goals is essential to achieving your dream. Remembering that your words have power creates a crescendo of fireworks. All it takes is for you to manifest it into life. We are all caterpillars that put in the work and eclipse into a beautiful butterfly. You did the work and now believe it when you cannot see it is having faith. When you achieve it, that is **GRACE**.

YOU WILL KNOW WHEN YOU ARE ON THE CORRECT PATH. YOU WILL FEEL IT!

LOVE
YOURSELF!

KEEP YOUR PLANS TO YOURSELF UNTIL YOU ACHIEVE THEM!

BE
KIND
ALWAYS!

SIGN UP FOR MY AUTHOR NEWSLETTER

Get exclusive access to Anita Fonteboa's new releases and tailored content for readers and writers.

HTTPS://ANITAFONTEBOA.COM

If this book has resonated with you, kindly show your support for the author by crafting a brief review on Amazon, Goodreads, Barnes & Noble and other retailers' websites. Your valuable feedback can make a significant impact!

Anita Fonteboa is a Queens, New York, author, and a first-generation Latina graduate. With a Bachelor of Science in Legal Science from John Jay College, Anita started blogging as QueensNYCMom in 2011. She now creates video content on Anita Inspires YouTube channel, and lifestyle content on her website, AnitaInspires.com. She also wants to inspire you to be better on her podcast, Anita Inspires. Her loves include her family, traveling, watching Hallmark movies, and reading.

LET'S CONNECT ON:

Website:	anitafonteboa.com and anitainspires.com
Instagram:	@AnitaFonteboa and @AnitaInspires
Facebook:	@AnitaFonteboaAuthor and @AnitaInspires
Twitter:	@AnitaFonteboa and @AnitaInspires
YouTube:	https://www.youtube.com/@AnitaFonteboa and https://www.youtube.com/@AnitaInspires
Threads:	@AnitaFonteboa
TikTok:	@AnitaFonteboa

Made in the USA
Middletown, DE
05 December 2023

43549305R00056